I Am
Omnipowerful

I Am Omnipowerful

The Most Powerful Person on Earth

DR. OTTO UMANA

iUniverse LLC
Bloomington

I AM OMNIPOWERFUL
The Most Powerful Person on Earth

iUniverse books may be ordered through booksellers or by contacting:

iUniverse LLC
1663 Liberty Drive
Bloomington, IN 47403
www.iuniverse.com
1-800-Authors (1-800-288-4677)

ISBN: 978-1-4917-0431-8 (sc)
ISBN: 978-1-4917-0432-5 (hc)
ISBN: 978-1-4917-0433-2 (e)

Library of Congress Control Number: 2013915719

Printed in the United States of America

iUniverse rev. date: 11/11/2013

Contents

To you who may be curious to know more about the most powerful person in the universe, those who have given up the search for answers to the yearning of their hearts, the young men and women who are tired of trying to make it on their own, and the men and women who are holding onto his unchanging hands.

You have searched me, Lord, and you know me. You know when I sit and when I rise; you perceive my thoughts from afar. You discern my going out and my lying down; you are familiar with all my ways. Before a word is on my tongue you, Lord, you know it completely.

Psalm 136:1–4 (NIV)

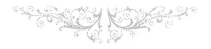

Acknowledgments

This book has evolved over several years. I am grateful for the encouragement and support by many. I thank Rev. Paul Eno, Dr. Mike Murdock, Bishop T. D. Jakes, and Dr. Miles Munroe. These men are shining lights and guardian angels. Without them, my time on earth would have been most boring, depressing, fruitless, and uneventful. Their prayers, dedication, commitment, and love to God have made the greatest impact on my life.

I love my wife, Kari, and sons, Michael and Joel, for their understanding and faithful support. Without the devotion to God and the children of my departed mother, Anthonia, and father, Damasus Joshua Umana, I would never have realized half of my dreams or potential. To my sister, Rosemary, and my brothers, Ini, Michael, and Mfon—I would never have completed my education without your love and generosity.

For the development and publication of this book, I feel a deep sense of gratitude to God and the Holy Spirit, who have been very patient with me from my days of disbelief until the time of this publication. To Richard Mabey Jr., my friend and writer—your encouragement and guidance have made this piece possible. To Austina Maree—your time and dedication to this book have expedited its completion.

Preface

I once met a wealthy man, Bishop Benson A. Idahosa. When he died, the press was curious to know how much money he left in his bank account. I do not know how the press got the information, but the amount was the equivalent of a hundred dollars. This man's investments in Africa amounted to more than fifty million in US dollars. He had invested all his money in schools, hospitals, churches, and housing for the people and built a university. His interest was in the lost, poor, and underprivileged primarily in Africa, but he worked in other parts of the world as well. Above all, he preached one message, "Faith in God, the one who can do the impossible."

The discoveries and advancements in medical science over the past twenty years are amazing. Nevertheless, the greatest bewilderment and amazement to me is the ancient of days, Jehovah God. His Word, as it is recorded in the Bible, has held its own for centuries. The wise men, philosophers, lawyers, politicians, and scientists have not been able to prove his words wrong. God does not need any randomized control trial to prove his Word. As a matter of fact, the first randomized control trial is recorded in Daniel 1, according to Marvin L. Hage, MD, a retired obstetrician in Wilmington, North Carolina.

When science records its changes and discoveries every day, God says, "I am the same yesterday, today, and forever" (Heb. 13:8 NIV). God is unchangeable, and immortal is dependable. He has not changed one of his words, but he has all the answers for the world's confusion and madness. God does not edit his Word. He spoke it once, and he has not shuffled or changed his mind. Despite our lack of knowledge about him, he has not changed his original plan for us, his creation. His plan for us, the men and women created in his own image, is love and perfect peace.

Some trust in money, education, fame, family, wealth, friends, connections, personal strength, beauty, eloquence, luck, intelligence, and power. In life, there are times when all these things fail us. At such times, we usually ask, "God, where are you?" For the past thirty years, I have been blessed to meet children, men, and women who had no one or nothing to trust in during desperate situations. After all the despair and pain, their last hope and savior has been God, the creator of the universe. "Some trust in chariots and some in horses, but we trust in the name of the Lord our God" (Ps. 20:7 NIV).

This book is a collection of true stories of men and women who trusted God, made him their refuge and strength, and thereby received answers to their prayers and miracles. I hope you will be encouraged to trust God more and have your faith in him strengthened as you read these stories. If I departed from the earth without sharing these testimonies, I would have robbed you of some of the knowledge of the power of God and robbed God of his glory.

Introduction

Amarillo, Texas (July 2000)

Colton was a forty-year-old former bouncer. He was Caucasian, aloof, and very convincing. He had witnessed many things during the United States Iraq–Kuwait War. He was quite muscular and could hold his own. He ignored me the whole time we worked together. One day, I was encouraging a work friend not to give up on his dreams. I was also telling him and other coworkers about the goodness of God. Coming from Nigeria, I had no inhibition about sharing my faith with anyone, regardless of his or her color or race.

Colton asked me a very interesting question in the middle of a conversation with other coworkers. "This God you have been speaking of, tell me. What have you seen him do personally? Forget the stories in the Bible, like the parting of the Red Sea."

The others asked, "If you think he exists, we want to hear about what he has done for you. What have you seen with your own eyes?"

Two of the men were homosexual; I knew the other one had never been to church. I do not know where the words came from. The events that laid the foundation for my faith in the supernatural began to flow slowly out of my belly with peace and certainty. I had never thought about them that way until Colton and his friends confronted me.

What I shared with them is in the first two chapters of this book. "Give thanks to the Lord, call on his name; make known among the nations what he has done" (Ps. 105:1 NIV). I decided to write this book after I came across several other men and women like Colton and his friend.

Chapter One

The Priceless Gem

My older brother Abasido was eleven. Tall, muscular, and handsome with dark curly hair, he was built well for his age. He was very funny. Others liked him, and he was the most useful person at home. He could cook, wash dishes, and do the laundry. When I was six, he taught me how to swim in a river after a near-drowning experience. He was so much fun to be with.

It was around seven twenty-five on a Monday morning, and we were supposed to be in school in five minutes. Arriving late to school would mean that we would be punished or have our teacher or school principal thrash us on the buttocks with a hard stick.

Fun Ride to School

Abasido had figured out that, if we came in through the front entrance of the school, we would be caught. Therefore, the only way we could avoid getting caught was to sneak in the back door and mix with other students. On this particular day, we were late that morning because our mother had prepared a special breakfast for us. It is called *dodokido*, and it is made with fried chopped overripe plantain. It is served with omelets prepared with eggs, fish or chicken, tomatoes, onions, salt, and a special seasoning. It was so yummy that we asked for more and could not get out of the house early.

Behind our elementary school was a small river, which Abasido was familiar with. He was required to do chores at home in the mornings, so he had figured out how not to get caught if he came late.

On this fateful morning, we had no ride to school, so we were all anxious and praying that we would not be caught coming in late. We had to walk for about ten to fifteen minutes to get to school. Abasido told us to follow him. He took us down a dirt road with birds singing and crickets jumping and chirping. In Abak, a small town in Nigeria, the bushes, trees, and lawns are always green no matter the time of year. We could see all kinds of natural beauty, flowers, and trees not planted by man; also, colorful birds and animals run around freely without fear in this area.

Walking down the dirt road, we finally arrived at a dead end, a small river. Abasido told us to take off all our clothes and shoes and put them in our school bags.

There were three of us brothers—Abasido, Michael, and myself. We were perplexed that Abasido would bring us to swim when we were supposed to be in school. He took my school bag from me and swam across the stream, which was about ten yards wide, with my bag in his left hand. He came back and told Michael and me to swim across the stream. To show off my swimming skills was such fun. I quickly dived in, and in no time, we were all on the other side of the river.

We waited for the water to dry off our bodies, and we got dressed. We went up a small dirt road, and within four minutes, we were in the school. We were not caught that day. It was so much fun that we decided to take the same way home after school, but we could not because my mother came to pick us up. No good deed goes unpunished.

Three weeks later, my teacher came to our home to visit, and he told my mother how we came to school through the back door. I guess we got the same punishment we had avoided earlier, the whip. This time, it was double what we would have had in school, but it was from our mother, not the teacher.

My mother was deeply disappointed. She was a no-nonsense woman, and for her, good grades were number one. Indiscipline was a number-one abomination. We got what we deserved and never went back to school by taking the beautiful dirt road.

Abasido Paralyzed

Twelve-year-old Abasido went to a boarding school for middle school. He was strong and energetic. One day, our family was given notice of the most devastating news that any family could have. We learned that Abasido had become paralyzed. He was home for the holidays and could not walk, move, or feel any sensation from his waist down.

Before Abasido's illness, my mother had been admitted to a hospital located about twenty-one miles from our house for severe abdominal pain. Abasido had been taking food to my mother from our home. The doctors had placed her on a special diet, which was not available at the hospital cafeteria. A chef had to prepare the meal at home, and Abasido and our driver took it to the hospital.

We were surprised to see our mother back home after five days of admission because we were told she might be in for more than a week. She had gone in as an emergency and left against medical advice upon hearing the news of Abasido's illness. She took Abasido from one hospital to the other, and it dragged from days to weeks and finally to months. All the tests in the hospitals were normal. Medical insurance was not available in this part of the world, as is the case in most developing countries. After spending so much money in hospitals, she decided to bring Abasido back home one day. Some people, including health-care workers, advised her that she should try the native healers.

She dragged Abasido from the most popular one to the greediest ones and spent more money, but Abasido still could not walk. Abasido was the second child in our family of five children. He was, however, the first male child and the most mysterious.

There was gloom, pain, and despair in our home. The funniest person in our family could not walk, run, or play games with us. My parents were distraught and confused. Mom had spent all her money and life savings on hospital bills. Finally, Abasido was admitted to one of the best hospitals in southeastern Nigeria for three weeks. But his condition worsened. After this admission and treatment, Mom decided to bring him home. She was sad, dejected, and desperate. My parents could hardly talk to each other. The once very happy family had fallen apart.

The Greatest Healer

Sobbing sounds coming from my parents' room woke us one morning. We rushed to the living room to find our mother, Abigail, in tears because she had a weird dream. In the dream, someone had told her, "How can you be sleeping when the most precious thing you have is dying? Get up and take your son to the church held at your children's elementary school, and there he will be healed."

We were all shocked, and we all thought she had gone crazy. Surprisingly, at five that same morning, my mother left for the school with Abasido. There she met with people she had never known to pray. Later that day, she told us that someone prophesying at the prayer meeting had asked her, "What did you come here for? To see the wind shaking the trees or to be helped by God?" Mom was told to go fast and pray with Abasido for one day with a promise to see the salvation of the Lord. She returned home around seven in the morning. There she showered, and then she took Abasido back to the church.

Surprisingly, Abasido came back home, walking with support. His muscles that had begun to atrophy regained their strength. Within a few days, we were trying out his legs with our new soccer ball. Joy had returned to our home. Another miracle had occurred in the town of Abak, where my mother worked as a registered nurse. Abasido is still alive today and can tell his story of the miracle that happened to him. Moreover, whereas our mother is no longer living, the power of God kept her faith and spirit alive. She had received the total package of salvation.

Some medical experts have argued with me that this was not a miracle. They suggested that Abasido could have had Guillain-Barré syndrome because it is associated with paralysis and spontaneous recovery in some patients.

It is amazing how Mom had a dream about where she should take Abasido for healing. Also, whatever the cause of the paralysis was, he did not die from the illness. Why did the dream, fasting, and healing occur on the same day? This is not a coincidence. Only the omnipowerful God and healer of our diseases can perform wonders like that. He wiped away the tears, sorrow, and depression that had crept into our home following our brother's paralysis. "Now to him who can do immeasurably more than all we ask or imagine, according to his power that is at work within us. To him be glory in the church and in Christ Jesus throughout all generations forever and ever! Amen" (Eph. 3:20–21 NIV).

During the preparations of this book, I believed that my brother would continue to receive the greatest miracle of all, the salvation that comes only from Jesus Christ. For some people, it takes time before they make the final decision and surrender to Jesus. Others wait until it is too late. I pray this will not be you. As you are reading this book, I do not know if you believe God exists or not. If you do, I pray you will be strengthened in the faith. If you have any doubt about the existence and power of God, I want you to pray this prayer with me. "Almighty God, I want to know you. Reveal yourself to me in Jesus's name. Amen."

For my mother, her son was her priceless gem until he became lame. God was ready to show her who the priceless gem Jesus Christ—the one who can step into our confusion, restlessness, hopelessness, sickness, disappointments, and disaster—is. "The thief comes only to steal and kill and destroy; I have come that they may have life, and have it to the full" (John 10:10 NIV). You can find this peace and tranquility in the midst of your storm.

Wise men do seek him, Jesus Christ, the priceless gem. Abasido's healing was one of the greatest miracles that our family witnessed in the city of Abak. We were blessed to witness other miracles made possible by the power of God.

Chapter Two

Transforming Power

"One thing God has spoken, two things I have heard: 'Power belongs to you, God'" (Ps. 62:11 NIV).

Greg the Dancer
Abak (1972)

Our family resided in Abak, a small city in Nigeria, from 1972 to 1974. I was smart, gentle, and fearless. I was only six, but I was willing to read anything. My most favorite thing was dancing. I represented my class at talent shows at the close of every school year. But I had terrible asthma attacks at the peak of my dancing performances and while exercising and during the spring.

The attacks were so bad for little me that I decided to quit talent shows at the end of my most recent performance. I had an older sister named Ruby who also suffered from asthma. Ruby was the first child. She was outgoing and unique in her own way.

Our mother had used all kinds of medication, both conventional and herbal. As long as I was not involved in high-speed dancing or running in cold weather, the asthma attacks were not so bad. Unfortunately for Ruby, she suffered more severe asthma attacks. She had been to see a doctor several times, and she was on three different medications.

On one Friday evening, four of us siblings had come back from school, and we all had eaten a very delicious meal made from pounded yam, chicken, and fish soup. After eating, our mother gave us an assignment for the weekend. She asked us to set traps for the red tree ants that had invaded some of the trees in our backyard. The person who caught the most ants would get a generous prize. We made several traps ranging from bags to large basins loaded with glue, sugar, candy, and cookies. Some of the traps were hung on tree branches; others were placed at the foot of the trees overnight.

After eating breakfast the following morning, Mom brought out a large pot filled with water and boiled it on the stove. Surprisingly, she did not prepare anything for the boiling water. She told us to gather our ant traps and bring them to her. Before we could step outside to get the ant traps, she sat down on the kitchen floor and started crying.

"What is wrong?" Ruby asked.

Mom told us that she was tired of what asthma was doing to her children. Between the two of us, Ruby and me, our mother would stay up many nights to care for us both.

Bug Juice

During the last hospital visit for Ruby's asthma, someone in the hospital told our mom to try a natural remedy, said to be the final cure for asthma. The remedy was to trap as many red tree ants as possible and boil them in a pot. And once the ants were filtered out, she would serve the "ant water" to us in a cup. She told her the drink was the final cure for asthma and many other diseases for her own children and relatives.

After telling the story, Mom cried so much that she could not stop. She was crying and praying for herself and her children at the same time.

She kept asking, "God, how can you let asthma afflict us so much? How can I give my children ant juice to drink when you are God and can do all things?"

After hearing the story, we were frightened. We consoled Mom, and my brothers and I slowly withdrew from the house to the backyard. Our mission was to burn all the ants because there was no way we were going to drink any bug juice. When Mom finally stopped sobbing, she asked us to get rid of the ants. We told her not to worry about it. The ants were already dead.

The Healing Crusade
Abak (1972)

After the bug juice incident, our mother decided to forget about herbs and trust in prescription medicines and God to take care of the asthma. She heard of a preacher who was coming to town and was said to have supernatural powers to heal the sick.

She decided to take all of us to a Christian crusade held in an open field in the town where we lived because my asthma attacks had gotten worse. At about seven thirty on a Friday evening, the speaker stood on the podium with a microphone in his hand. He was distinct from every other person in the crowd because he was not African. He had brown curly hair, and he was probably in his midforties.

The crusade had been publicized in the local newspaper and announced in all the schools and churches in the town. About two thousand people gathered for the meeting.

The speaker said, "If you are sick in any part of your body, touch it with your hands."

And he prayed a simple prayer. We experienced so much peace, contentment, and joy. Shouts of shock, joy, and disbelief disrupted the peace, calm, and quiet. A blind man in the crowd regained his sight. A disabled man crippled from birth received strength from the supernatural. He got out of his wheelchair and walked. Both men were well known because their means of sustenance was begging for alms. They received their healing along with many others touched by that supernatural power.

I had put my hand on my chest when this man prayed. I have not experienced any attack of asthma since I met this man and encountered the supernatural. Some doctors have told me that I had childhood asthma and it went away by itself. This might be true, but why did it suddenly disappear the night Dr. T. L. Osborne prayed for me? Although he came to Abak in 1972 when I was only six, I cannot forget his name because he came with the supernatural that touched and transformed many lives and left a lasting impression in my life.

About six months prior to Dr. Osborne's visit to Abak, the citizens of that city were made to stand on the streets and wave flags to receive the military ruler of Nigeria, General Yakubu Gowon. General Gowon visited Abak with a large entourage and promised to build a stadium in our state capitol and introduce tuition-free education at the elementary school level.

Although the general's visit to my hometown was memorable, my personal encounter with the supernatural caught my attention more than coming close to the very nice and handsome Nigerian military ruler. During his meeting in Abak, Dr. Osborne spoke of nothing besides Jesus and his ability to deliver and set free people. After witnessing the miracles mentioned above, I thought of Dr. Osborne as a very powerful man from heaven.

In 1989, seventeen years later, I finally understood where his power came from. Jesus Christ, during his final fleshly encounter with his disciples, had told them, "Go into the world and preach the gospel to all creation" (Mark 16:15 NIV).

> Whoever believes and is baptized will be saved, but whoever does not believe will be condemned. These signs will accompany those who believe: In my name they will drive out demons; they will speak in new tongues; they will pick up snakes with their hands, and they will drink deadly poison, it will not hurt them at all; they will place their hands on sick people, and they will get well. (Mark 16:16–19 NIV)

I perceive that Dr. T. L Osborne obeyed the Word of God just as it is written in the Bible. God does not waste words. He backed up his Word just as he promised in the book of Isaiah.

> As the rain and the snow come down from heaven, and do not return to it without watering the earth and making it bud and flourish, so that it yields seed for the sower and bread for the eater, so is my word that goes out from my mouth: It will not return to me empty, but accomplish what I desire and achieve the purpose for which I sent it. (Isa. 55:10–11 NIV)

Salvation

During the encounter with Dr. Osborne, some people received the total package of salvation. The noun "salvation" has four meanings: the act of delivering from sin or saving from evil, a means of preserving from harm or unpleasantness, the state of being preserved from harm, or saving someone or something from harm or from an unpleasant situation. "Redemption" is a synonym.

Salvation comes from the Greek word SOZO. A simple meaning of SOZO is "rescued," "pulled from danger," or, in Ephesians 2:8, "by Grace you are saved" (NIV). Redemption's definition includes salvation, healing, and deliverance. SOZO describes God's awesome plan to change our lives inside and out and includes transforming the spirit, soul, and body.

Jesus the Lord is salvation. He can deliver, heal, set free, and preserve from all kinds of disease and situations. Is it depression, abuse, neglect, rejection, cancer, heart disease, loneliness, frustration, poverty, shame, lack of wisdom, failure, drug dependence, or pride? Jesus said, "The thief comes only to steal and kill and destroy: I have come that they may have life and have it to the full" (John 10:10 NIV).

We do have temporary fixes to many of our problems. We turn to the use of alcohol and drugs and prescription medications such as in Xanax, Vicodin, and Ritalin. We even use different kinds of therapy, exercise, and other mind-control nonhealers. Although these medications and temporary solutions have their genuine uses and benefits, I am surprised how the problems never seem to go away completely. After the medication is out of the system, people always go back for more.

In John 10:10, Jesus promises to give life richer and fuller because it is full of love, forgiveness, and guidance. Could it be that the source of some of our health problems is not just physical but the presence of the devil? Acts 10:38 records how God anointed Jesus of Nazareth with the Holy Spirit and power and how Jesus went around doing good and healing all who were under the power of the devil because God was with him.

In the first two chapters, I have given an eyewitness account of some of the miracles I saw as a child, demonstrations of God's supernatural healing power. Could it be that this healing by the power of God is available for all who ask for it? How did we live for so many years without knowing about the Internet? Is it possible that we are spiritually blind? Is there any such thing as spiritual blindness? Could it be surgically corrected?

Chapter Three

Blindness

Amaka was a tough thirty-eight-year-old woman from the town of Calabar, which sits on the southeastern side of Nigeria. Mbaseki, Amaka's husband, was a nice man who was easygoing, funny, and well rounded. One would believe that Amaka had everything she could desire in a man. The only thing missing in their lives was conceiving a child. According to the culture in this bubbling town of Calabar, a family's joy was incomplete without a child. Mbaseki was the man of Amaka's dreams, and he truly loved Amaka. One could tell this by life that radiated from him to others and his faithfulness to his wife. Both were well educated, upper class, and well respected in their community.

Not being able to conceive a child was puzzling for Amaka. She speculated that something must be wrong. Amaka knew that the average onset for a female menstrual cycle had to occur in the teenage years. Because she hadn't seen her first menstrual period over the years, Amaka knew this was much more than her age. She had everything needed to qualify one physiologically and anatomically as a woman, including a uterus and ovaries. After several visits to doctors, laboratory testing, medications, and injections, the results still confused Amaka.

Mbaseki understood the situation; however, he was already forty years old. He had become more concerned and worried. In Africa, a longtime tradition is for a married couple to have a child so their parents can enjoy grandparenting. Figuratively speaking, Mbaseki tried to make the best of Amaka's issue with conceiving by supporting and believing that his wife would be with child one day. However, Amaka did not have faith. Nor did she believe in God.

Amaka was like some others whom I have encountered in Nigeria and other parts of the world that do not believe in God. Some individuals believe in the existence of the devil, but they do not believe that God exists. They are blind like Amaka, and like Amaka, she had to rotate her thoughts on what disbelief is and align it with the truth to see what God is capable of doing for her.

The Paradox

In 2 Kings 5:1–14, Naaman, the captain of the Syrian army, had leprosy, and a slave girl from Israel told him to see a prophet from Samaria for a cure. When he reluctantly visited the prophet Elisha, Naaman was told to bathe in the Jordan River for cleansing. The general was angry and did not want to go. It sounded more like a joke or insult. He clearly was against going.

But Naaman went away angry and said, "I thought he would surely come out to me and stand and call on the name of the Lord his God, wave his hand over the spot, and cure me of my leprosy. Are not Aban and Pharpar, the rivers of Damascus, better than all the waters of Israel? Couldn't I wash in them and be cleansed?"

So he turned and went off in rage in 2 Kings 5:11–12.

The Jordan River

Naaman was spiritually blind outright. In both the Old and New Testaments, many miracles took place at the Jordan River. Naaman described Aban and Pharpar as better rivers than all those in Israel. The Jordan River is said to be the source of life for the surrounding lands referred to as the garden of God. The prophet Elisha had spiritual insight. He remembered what happened when he crossed the Jordan River with his master and mentor Elijah (Yardenit. "Yardenit Jordan River," www.yardenit.com/? section=80&item=124).

The river is mentioned 175 times in the Old Testament and 15 times in the New Testament. Naaman had no spiritual insight. He considered the Jordan River inferior to rivers he knew back in his home. When he humbled himself and obeyed the prophet and Word of God, he received healing and revelation of the power of the God of Israel.

Naaman was not the only person who was spiritually blind. So was Gehazi, Elisha's servant. Elisha prayed to God to open the spiritual eyes of his servant so he may see the chariots of fire protecting them in 2 Kings 6:8–17.

Let us look at the paradox concerning Amaka. The recommendation for treatment of the commander of the Syrian army came from a captive slave girl from Israel. She wanted him to visit a captive prophet for healing of leprosy. The prophet refused payment for treatment, but he wanted him to bathe in a shabby river for healing.

Conception

Amaka found herself in this kind of paradox. She was educated and upper class and she did not believe in God. A born-again Christian told her to visit the pastor of one of those new churches for prayers. She was thirty-eight without ever seeing her menstrual period; her ovaries were said to be nonfunctional. Amaka and her doctors had given up hope about conception. She was told that her only hope for conception and childbearing was a miracle from God. As a last resort, Amaka reluctantly went and visited the pastor who was recommended to her for prayers.

He was well known for his boasts in the power of God. Amaka said, "I had never seen a menstrual period until I went to Reverend Edikan to pray for me." Within a few days of prayer, Amaka saw her menstrual period for the first time. She conceived and gave birth to a healthy baby boy. She said to me that, although she had a period for the first time in her life and had a child, she still did not believe in God. Like many individuals in this world, Amaka is spiritually blind. "God is awesome; he makes the sun to shine on both the believers and unbelievers" (2 Cor. 10:3–4 NIV).

Paul the apostle was spiritually blind. One day, he had the scales fall out from his eyes. He wrote the following verse according to the inspiration of the Holy Spirit.

> But even if our Gospel (the glad tidings) also be hidden (obscured and covered up with a veil that hinders the knowledge of God), it is hidden [only] to those who are perishing and obscured [only] to those who are spiritually dying and veiled [only] to those who are lost. For the god of this world has blinded the unbelievers' minds [that they should not discern the truth],

preventing them from seeing the illuminating light of the Gospel of the glory of Christ (the Messiah), who is the Image and Likeness of God. (2 Cor. 4:3–4 AB)

Amaka is not the only one caught up in this web of disbelief. I have met several people who do not believe in God and question his existence, and they are completely wrapped up in what they see in this world. Some will like to feel the nails in his hands first and to see the cross on which he was crucified. In addition, some would want to see Noah's ark before they are convinced of his existence. I am positive that you have also met several people like Amaka, or you yourself perhaps may have relatives who have chosen to believe in evolution or want a randomized control trial before they will believe and come to worship their creator and Lord.

Guess what? God loves us as he does Amaka unconditionally, even when we have chosen not to believe in him. Why should God care? one may ask. Just as a good father cares for his children much more so, God cares for us more than we will ever know in this life. His love and heart are larger than yours and mine. "'For my thoughts are not your thoughts, neither are your ways my ways,' declares the Lord. 'As the heavens are higher than the earth, so are my ways higher than your ways and my thoughts your thoughts'" (Isa. 55:8–9 NIV). This is why we marvel at his beauty and holiness. Almighty God loves us in spite of our sins, unbelief, and shortcomings.

We all have the same disease: spiritual blindness. We doubt God and trust only in what we see, hear, and have. We have lost hope and not searched for more. God told the people of Israel, "My people are destroyed for lack of knowledge. Because you have rejected knowledge, I also reject you as my priests; because you have ignored the law of your God, I also will ignore your children" (Hos. 4:6 AMP).

Let us put it another way. If I wanted to know about the Toyota Company, the manufacturer of my car, I would not go to my garage and ask the car. I would go to Japan. I may have to second-guess these travels plans without enough sky miles. So taking a tour in a plant in the United States would better suffice. Then again, I could take an online course while there are plenty to choose from nowadays. So what makes Toyota cars such nice and durable vehicles? The price, looks, or energy efficiency? Or is it the name?

Keep Searching for the Truth

Amaka's story and the Toyota Company are based on the mere thoughts of you doubting the power and existence of God. I will encourage you to ask God to show himself to you. If you know of anybody who does not believe or has doubt, I ask that you pray for him or her. Pray that God will open his or her blind eyes so he or she can see and know who his or her creator is and begin to enjoy the benefits of knowing him.

It is amazing how people who have not read the Bible before and do not have the belief that Jesus Christ is the Son of God will readily believe historical and scientific inaccuracies like *The Da Vinci Code* by Dan Brown. The Bible is the most interesting book ever written. The Word of God has the power to transform, heal, and set people free from all kinds of blindness and bondages. The best source of wisdom, peace, and power is the Word of God. It is better than silver or gold.

Most people will not read it, and some will never know who God really is. If you have never read the Bible, I will encourage you to read John 1–3, meditate on it, and ask questions. Search for a Bible with commentaries and pray to God to show you who he and Jesus are.

People are living in denial of who God is. Some others fear what others will say or think of them if they publicly proclaim their belief and knowledge of God. It does not matter what your fear is. I want you to know what God thinks about you. He loves you so much that he made you in his own image. The love he has for us compelled him to send his Son to die for you and me so our sins would be forgiven and we may have a relationship with him.

Chapter Four

Unconditional Love

Unconditional love is not something we compete for. Nor is it something to be earned. It is the greatest definition of God. I was nine years old at the top of my class in school and going off to a boarding school. As a child, I thought the only persons obligated to love you were your mother and father because that kind of love is difficult to compete with.

Most things come by privilege, but the love of God and my parents was unconditional, and unconditional love is not something that has to be earned. When I was nine, my mother instructed me to "go to church like every other student but not associate with those weird born-again Christians." She was referring to some Christians who did not think it was right for women to have their hair uncovered or to wear jewelry and makeup.

When I got to school, I met Christians like that at least once every week. They were generally nice. Some would buy lunch, and they would start preaching.

"If you do not repent, you will go to hell."

I would say, "Why do you think or say so?"

They would reply, "The Bible says the soul that sinneth shall die."

I used to smile and sometimes laugh at them. "You are preaching to the wrong person. I really know God, and you do not need to worry about me."

How could they tell me that I did not know God or I was going to hell when I had been healed at the age of six and seen God heal blind, deaf, and lame men? What should I have repented from when I was a good boy, did not tell lies, and did not get into any trouble in school? I continued to run into this kind of people at least once a month during my high school and college days.

My reply was the same. "I do not womanize, smoke, tell lies, or steal from anyone. So why do you think I should perish?"

The scales fell out of my eyes one day at a crusade held at the University of Benin, Nigeria. The Anglican Church youth fellowship organized it.

Benin (May 1989)

There were two real churches at the University of Benin. The other one was a Catholic church.

My father was a faithful Catholic member. Handsome and quiet, he enjoyed drinking beer. He told me when I had admission to this institution, "If you see other students go to church and read the Bible, I want you to do the same."

The crusade was held on a Saturday evening in May 1989. The preacher, Reverend Onibere, was a lecturer at the University of Ife, and the Anglican youth fellowship had invited him. My intelligent, devout, and God-fearing friend Marna invited me to the crusade. The week prior to the crusade had been tragic for everyone in the university community. The university staff members and students had mourned the loss of a member of the academic community,

Professor Benjamin, a respected physician and professor in the department of medicine.

Free at Last

After a peaceful and well-attended funeral service, we all gathered at the crusade ground around seven o'clock in the evening. Reverend Onibere came to the podium after the initial prayers, praise, and worship. His concise message was that we were all born sinners. We all inherited sin from Adam, which manifests itself in different ways. He referred to verses in the Bible showing that God loves us and made a plan to reconcile us back to himself. "In fact the law requires that nearly everything be cleansed with blood, and without the shedding of blood there is no forgiveness of sin" (Heb. 9:22 NIV). Jesus Christ died and shed his blood for our sins. God sent his Son Jesus Christ to pay the penalty for our sins. Jesus has reconciled us to God through his sacrifice. If we acknowledge who we are and accept the love of Christ, then we are accepted and reconciled to God our creator. It does not matter how good you are. If you shall die today and you do not know and have not accepted Jesus, you will go to hell.

He sympathized with the university community concerning the loss of our dear professor. He simply acknowledged Professor Benjamin as a nice and caring husband and father, professor, and good man. If he did not know and had not accepted Jesus as his Lord and Savior, he would not be accepted into heaven. I had been to church one hundred times, but I had not heard it that way. At the age of twenty-two, I wrestled with this revelation knowledge, which was quite different from what I had heard in the church I attended regularly. Better stated, my spiritual eyes were opened, as I saw Jesus and only him as the one who paid the price for us to go to heaven. During the altar call, I decided to go up to the stage with my eyes closed to accept Jesus, the only way to heaven, along with several others, among them professors who taught at my school.

My eyes were closed, as I did not want anything or anyone to discourage me nor give me odd looks or glances. I needed Jesus Christ that night to hear my cry, forgive my sins, and accept me into the beloved. This night marked the beginning of a new chapter in my life. I became more curious about God and his love for us. I was taught according to the Bible.

"But you are a chosen people, a royal priesthood, a holy nation, God's special possession, that you may declare the praises of him who called you out of darkness into his wonderful light" (1 Pet. 2:9 NIV). It was not long before I started doubting the new creation that I was taught I had become in Christ. I had the same body and mind, and by this time, I became more aware of some desires common to people my age. The puzzle was solved three years later when I surrendered myself to teaching in a new convert's class.

What the Bible Says about Sin

In Romans 5:12–21 (NIV), it states,

> Therefore, just as sin entered the world through one man, and death through sin, and in this way death came to all people because all sinned—To be sure, sin was in the world before the law was given, but sin is not charged against anyone's account where there is no law. Nevertheless, death reigned from the time of Adam to the time of Moses, even over those who did not sin by

breaking a command, as did Adam, who is a pattern of the one to come. But the gift is not like the trespass. For if the many died by the trespass of the one man, how much more did God's grace and the gift that came by the grace of the one man, Jesus Christ, overflow to the many! Nor can the gift of God be compared with the result of one man's sin: The judgment followed one sin and brought condemnation, but the gift followed many trespasses and brought justification. For if, by the trespass of the one man, death reigned through that one man, how much more will those who receive God's abundant provision of grace and of the gift of righteousness reign in life through the one man, Jesus Christ! Consequently, just as one trespass resulted in condemnation for all people, so also one righteous act resulted in justification and life for all people. For just as through the disobedience of the one man the many were made sinners, so also through the obedience of the one man the many will be made righteous. The law was brought in so that the trespass may increase. But where sin increased, grace increased all the more, so that, just as sin reigned in death, so also grace might reign through righteousness to bring eternal life through Jesus Christ our Lord.

God's love for us is everlasting and unconditional. Only our Father who created us in his own image could do this. God is saying to you today, "I know who you are and what you do daily, but my son has paid the price for you." My own image . . . I love you . . . I understand you feel far away, guilty, rotten, and filthy. The blood of

Jesus Christ has been accepted on your behalf. You have eternal life. Accept the unconditional love of God today.

The Greatest Miracle of All

According to Romans 5, we were all born into sin. The sin we inherited from Adam manifests itself in different ways: lies, stealing, drunkenness, adultery, fornication, greed, rage, murder, and so forth. The only way we can be made righteous or whole again is to accept the bloodshed sacrifice of Jesus Christ, the Son of God. It does not matter how much good work you do. Jesus said, "For God so loved the world that he gave his only Son that whoever believes in him shall not perish but have eternal life" (John 3:16 NIV).

God did not send his Son into the world to condemn the world but to save the world through him. This is the greatest miracle anyone can receive. You do not have to do anything but tell God who you are and accept Jesus into your life. I received this miracle in 1989. The miracle is free and yours. This is the gateway to love, peace, joy, miracles, and, above all, eternal life.

A Simple Prayer

Ask Jesus to forgive your sins and to give you the Holy Spirit, the one who will guide you from today until you are united with Jesus. You are forgiven, and you have eternal life. Receive the Holy Spirit in Jesus's name. Amen.

This single revelation of our old nature and transformation into new people is greater than silver or gold. If you prayed this prayer, know that now you are no longer alone. You are adopted as God's child through Jesus Christ.

The Holy Spirit, teacher, and guide are always with you. He will show you who God your Father is and the height, depth, and breadth of the love of Jesus. Jesus said, "I will never leave you nor forsake you. It is expedient that I go away and I will send you the Holy Spirit, the comforter who will guide you into all truths." Brethren, you are loaded with life and power from God.

When you reconnect to Elohim your maker, you will realize who you really are, and you will go through this life without fear. Fear not. You are not alone. You have backup from heaven. Confront your goals, problems, and obstacles to the best of your ability.

How excellent is the love the Father has lavished on us that we should be called children of God. That is what we are. The reason the world does not know us is that it did not know him. Dear friends, we are children of God, and what we will be has not yet been made known. Nevertheless, we know that when he appears, we shall be like him, for we shall see him as he is. "Everyone who has this hope in him purifies himself, just as he is pure" (1 John 3:1–3 NIV).

Chapter Five

Overcome Your Fears

Musa, Uyo Market (1996)

Fear filled Musa. He owned a large boutique along with others from his hometown. To succeed in his kind of business, some said one had to make sacrifices to the devil or visit those who practice voodoo. Musa was married to his wife Olivia, and together, they had a nine-year-old son. He sold men's and women's clothing, shoes, and jewelry in his boutique. I had not seen Musa in church for about a month, so I decided to visit him at his boutique one evening. When I arrived at his store, there were not many customers, so he had time to sit down and chat with me.

He narrated his story to me. His business was failing because of multiple reasons that he didn't care to discuss. He told me that he did not know what to do. He had trusted God for so many years. Now, his business and family were falling apart. He had no money to pay his mortgage, his children's school fees, or his workers. His plan was to close the business and move to his village to do God knows what. He had already assumed he was a failure.

I was worried for Musa, as he was a likable man who was typically positive and not like his fellow merchants. A percentage of the merchants who worked in the same area of business as Musa did not know or fear God. They loved and trusted in money and believed it was the only thing that mattered. I had known Musa for over two years and had never seen him unhappy, sad, or without hope. Musa was always full of joy. One could never tell he had a problem. I was full of trust and confidence in God at that time and believed that there was nothing God could not do through us if we asked.

I asked him about his car, and he said he wanted to sell it because he could no longer maintain it. Unfortunately for him, no one was willing to buy the car at the time. A few days later, I found a friend who had some money saved up and was looking for a car to purchase. He was the answer to part of Musa's problems. He bought the car within forty-eight hours of seeing it. Musa invested the money in his business and forgot about closing it down.

His business was just part of his problems. His wife, Olivia, wanted more children, and after trying to conceive for nine years, she still was not with child. For the first time, she decided to leave town and go to a women's conference in Benin City, Nigeria. The late Archbishop Benson Idahosa held the conference at Church of God Mission International. Three months after the conference, Musa's wife was pregnant with twins. I delivered the twin babies, and I was filled with amazement at the wonders of God when I heard of Olivia's testimony.

I heard this testimony in the church about sixteen months after the delivery. She gave a testimony in front of a church of more than seven hundred people. She told everyone how she was not able to get pregnant for nine years. She had been to several doctors and spent a substantial amount of money without any success. She got pregnant after attending the women's conference held at the Church of God Mission in Benin, Nigeria.

She was going back to Benin for another conference and was inviting other women to the conference because she believed that the power of God at the conference could heal and deliver people and set them free. A year after her second conference, she gave birth to her fourth child, a daughter named Marvella, meaning "miracle."

Have Faith in God

Olivia refused to believe medical doctors' reports on not being able to conceive. Refusing to sit down and accept defeat, she was certainly not ready to give up. She eventually overcame all her fears and stepped out in faith to receive the seed of faith, which propelled her body to ovulate and conceive. This is not all that happened to this couple. She started her own business by selling fast food that became very popular among the citizens and tourists who came to the small town of Uyo.

Musa was full of fear when I met him. I could read fear, frustration, and defeat in every word he spoke. I knew the God we served, and I refused to accept defeat too. God is always a step ahead of us. He is so smart and all knowing. You need to connect with him now. For the first time in your life, quit trying to fix everything by yourself. Accept who you are, and exchange your fears and imperfections with the supernatural.

In exchange, receive the supernatural wisdom from God that connected with Musa and his wife, which helped them both take a bold step of faith and received their hearts' desires. The God we serve can do the impossible. He created the world from nothing and said, "The just shall live by faith" (Heb. 10:38 NIV).

God is saying to those of us who may be tired, weary, sick, and dejected,

Fear not, for I have redeemed you; I have summoned you by name; you are mine. When you pass through the waters, I will be with you; and when you pass through the rivers, they will not sweep over you. When you walk through the fire, you will not be burned; the flames will not set you ablaze. For I am the LORD, your God, the Holy One of Israel, your Savior; since you are precious and honored in my sight, and because I love you, I will give men in exchange for you, and people in exchange for your life. Do not be afraid, for I am with you; I will bring your children from the east and gather you from the west. (Isa. 43:1–5 NIV)

Lions Have No Fear

Since the September 11, 2001, terrorist attacks that affected Americans and others across the nation, I have met so many people who are terrified and tremble at the mere mention of the word "terrorist." Terrorism is a violent attack intended to create fear. September 11 was a wake-up call to everyone in the world. We now know that we are not invincible. We need to expect the unexpected, prepare for the future, and be ready for anything. Sometimes the difference between being alive and being dead is a few minutes.

I want to encourage you not to fear him who can destroy the flesh but who can destroy both the flesh and spirit. Trust in the Lord with all your heart, and lean not on your own understanding.

This kind of trust does not come from attending church on a Sunday. It comes from taking your own Bible, sitting at his feet daily, and studying it with prayer. A simple prayer, for instance, says, "God, I want to know you more."

While I know you are busy and do not have much free time, you can take a few minutes away from the television. This would be the time to reflect on getting to know God. God told Joshua, "Do not let this Book of Law depart from your mouth; meditate on it day and night, so that you may be careful to do everything written in it. Then you will be prosperous and successful" (Josh. 1:8 NIV).

Faith comes from hearing, and hearing comes from the Word of God. Fear also comes from listening to negative information. Sometimes, our state of mind, depression, and confusion are a sum of the information received from men and processed in the mind without consulting our creator.

Jesus Christ is also known as the Lion of the Tribe of Judah. If you are a Christian, you have the DNA of Christ; you have the DNA of the Lion of the Tribe of Judah. Begin to believe, think, and live like your maker. You were created in God's image. Have you ever heard of God being scared?

Connect to a Bible-teaching and spirit-filled church. Spend time there, search the Bible for yourself, and pray to the Holy Spirit for understanding. Change your circle of friends, and allow the Holy Spirit to teach you. Remember Jesus said that, when the Holy Spirit comes, he will guide you into all truths. Put your trust in him, and have expectations. Do not live life hopeless, but trust in God to answer your prayers.

To me, the word "impossible" means unbelief. Jesus told his disciples, "With man this is impossible but with God all things are possible" (Matt. 19:26 NIV). I have eliminated this word from my thought process and vocabulary. Do not just sit there; get up and move toward your goal, do your best, and see God complete it. Break free of your fears. I was once a victim of fear and torment. Thank God that I am free today.

Chapter Six

Free Yourself

Fear and Torment (1995–1997)

How could Daniel trust God so much that he was willing to go to the lion's den? Why is it so different now? Are signs for unbelievers? Why do miracles occur in Africa and not America? Many people have asked these questions when they hear about the goodness and power of our Almighty God Jehovah Shammah. I do not know all the answers, but I will tell you a little about what I have seen. Miracles do occur in America too. You can never know or experience the power of God if you do not spend time with him.

As a bachelor pursuing my tropical rotation (clinical rotation) in Africa, I found myself lonely at times and in search of something other than medical knowledge, books, and adventure. There was an emptiness that I knew I could not fill. One weekend in the fall of 1994, I decided to visit one church in town. During the meeting, someone told me that evil people had determined that I would be dead by the end of the year. Evil powers were going to kill me. This was not said quietly one-on-one, but it was a prophecy with the whole church listening. There was no explanation for this evil plan. They did not say what I did wrong and did not provide a way of escape.

I left the church feeling sad, dejected, confused, and full of fear. I was so worried that I could not sleep at night and could not help but reflect on my life and the way I was living. I decided to get out of town before the end of the year. I was getting angry because, in my mind, I had tried to live right. I did not purposely offend anybody, I was working as hard as possible in my chosen career, and I did not understand what I had done to offend people, the devil, or God that deserved death. I had spent my whole life in church as a Christian, and I was defenseless, scared, and tormented by the fear of people planning to kill me.

The Blame Game

The culture in some parts of Africa has an explanation for everything. Every mishap is blamed on your enemies. If you have a headache, you can blame it on your cousin who does not like you. You can tell he really dislikes you because he did not say hello to you the last time you saw him at the family reunion. If the people are really generous, they will say it is the devil using your cousin. It goes deeper. If someone has a miscarriage, she will most likely blame it on the mother-in-law or oldest living family member.

The wrongfully blamed person is usually labeled as practicing witchcraft or voodoo. The more serious the illness, the more likely people are to blame problems on an older relative or someone he or she does not like. Some individuals growing up in Africa are brainwashed with this kind of belief that causes so much fear, separation, and hatred between families. The worst part of it is that people live with so much fear of witchcraft, voodoo, and the devil. This kind of fear is partly a result of numerous stories being told everywhere about the wicked acts of witches, voodoo, and the devil.

The fear is as crippling as the fear of developing cancer. This was my state after I was told that the kingdom of darkness had decided that I had a few months to live.

But Where Is God?

The following morning and over subsequent weeks, I had one question in my head. If God truly exists and he is the creator of all humanity, heaven, and earth, why would he allow the devil to torment my life? Is God more powerful than the devil? Did his Son truly die on the cross to deliver us from all evil? Is the devil, witchcraft, or voodoo more powerful than God's power? I knew I had done nothing wrong to deserve death. God has always protected me. I have never had this problem. I needed an answer. I started praying to God on my own and seeking answers.

The answer came before long through an invitation to a church for a friend's child dedication. Ordinarily, I was quite busy and did not have time for such invitations. Sean Joseph was my classmate in high school. We were not close friends back then, but he was humble, smart, and very funny while we were in school. You could not help but like him, and we got along well. I decided to go to his child's dedication because I had not seen him since high school graduation, more than eight years prior.

An attorney, he was married and dedicated to his family. He was very brilliant and seemed to make the right choices while we were together in school. He had become a born-again Christian, and he was a member of a new church called Church of God Mission International in Uyo. This church was so different from those I had ever been to. The music from the worship team was excellent.

The well-dressed people were full of joy. There was peace in the atmosphere, and people praised God with their hands lifted up.

The most interesting part of the worship service was the pastor's message. Rev. Paul Eno preached that day with such passion and enthusiasm about the power of God. He was totally convinced that God Almighty was most powerful and no voodoo, witchcraft, or devil could contend with God. He said something I had never heard all my life. He openly challenged witches, voodoo, and the devil. He announced his home address and made an open invitation to the witches and devil to visit his house and kill him if they had more power than God did.

Spiritual Eyes Opened

In my mind, I had found the right church, one where people were promoting the power of God, not the power of evil. I started going to Reverend Eno's church from that day. The Sunday following the child dedication service, he made another very interesting statement at closing. He said, "If I pastor you for a year and you do not see a change in your life, know that there is something seriously wrong with you." It was not long after I joined this church that I learned more about God and a prayer from a verse of scripture that totally blew my mind and changed my life forever.

Thanksgiving and Prayer from Paul the Apostle

In the book of Ephesians, it states that God raised Jesus from the dead and gave him authority, power, and dominion above everything. He had also placed everything under his feet. Apostle Paul's prayer was that God would give the church the spirit of wisdom and revelation so we may know God better, what he has in store for us, and the power he has deposited in us. The same power that conquered the grave and raised Jesus from the dead is deposited in those who believe in him.

> For this reason ever since I heard about your faith in the Lord Jesus and your love for all God's people, I have not stopped giving thanks for you, remembering you in my prayers. I keep asking that the God of our Lord Jesus Christ, the glorious Father, may give you the Spirit of wisdom and revelation, so that you may know him better. I pray that the eyes of your heart may be enlightened in order that you may know the hope to which he has called you, the riches of his glorious inheritance in his holy people, and his incomparably great power for us who believe. (Eph. 1:15–19 NIV)

> That power is the same as the mighty strength,

> He exerted when he raised Christ from the dead and seated him at his right hand in heavenly realms, far above all rule and authority, power and dominion, and every name that is invoked not only in the present age but also in the one to come. God placed all things under his feet and appointed him to be head over everything for the church, which is his body, the fullness of him who fills everything in every way. (Eph. 1:20–23 NIV)

The Scales Fell Out of My Eyes

Fear enslaved me, as it enslaves so many people today. I would state that up to 75 percent of people in some cultures are enslaved by this kind of fear unless they have come to the full revelation knowledge of God.

It was a week of fasting and prayers in the church. Reverend Eno encouraged us to pray the prayer from Paul the apostle every day that week for ourselves and loved ones. During one of the teaching, fasting, and prayer sessions, I received the Word of God that drove away the fear of the devil. Reading and meditating on Ephesians 1:15–23 (NIV) revealed the power of God, driving away the stronghold and bondage of fear in my life. It was as if a lightbulb had exploded in my head and mind, blowing away years of fear.

It was not long before I began to read the Bible and embrace the goodness and power of God. The fear of death, witches, witchcrafts, voodoo, and evil soon faded away. I was free from bondage and torment of the fear of evil. I could not help but study the Bible, go to Bible classes, and soon begin to tell others about the goodness and power of God. This might seem like a small thing in some people's opinion. However, this was a breakthrough for my family. My mother, who this kind of fear also tore apart, soon embraced the power of God and overcame her fear of evil.

Different kinds of fear—the fear of cancer, diabetes, addictions, losing your job, divorce, bankruptcy, or dying—torment so many people. I will encourage you to draw closer to God and his Son, Jesus Christ, the head of all things. He will help you overcome your fears and make your life whole again. His Word says, "Greater is he that is in us than he that is in the world" (1 John 4:4).

God used this experience to teach me how to discern between lies told by man and the voice of God. I no longer accept people's reports about me without checking with the Word of God. When God speaks, he brings peace, life, deliverance, unity, and solutions. He is not the author of fear, confusion, stress, and pain. People and the devil cause fear, confusion, pain, and stress. If the people who prophesied were right about someone planning to kill me, guess what? I am still alive today, and the devil is no match for the power of God. Your peace will depend on who you are listening to, the Word of God or the word of man.

Spiritual Growth

Reverend Eno once told me that one hindrance to knowing God more was something that we already have from all the education we have been filled with. I spent several hours at least three times every week studying the Word of God, praying and worshipping with this man and other believers. The Wednesday Bible teaching was where I began to receive an in-depth understanding of the power and wisdom of God. He shared with us deep secrets of the kingdom of God, something you cannot receive in a Sunday service. We used to spend at least four hours in the church on Sunday mornings: one hour in Sunday school, one hour praising and worshipping, and one hour for the Word of God.

Wednesday evening was Bible teaching, thirty minutes of praise and worship, and at least one hour of teaching. Thursday evening was men's fellowship. It lasted for at least an hour. I was a bachelor at this time, but here I learned a lot about being a good husband and father. Weekend fire fellowship was something one could not afford to miss. This meeting lasted for three hours on three consecutive days.

Some of us went to such meetings fasting, ready to receive guidance to help at our jobs and solutions to problems that human wisdom could not solve. Men received healing; some were freed from the bondage of alcoholism, drug abuse, whoring, and pornography. There is no defined time, minute, or hour that we have to spend to experience and see the power of God. The key is to seek God with all our heart, mind, and soul, and all other things will follow.

Today in America, we are too interested in other things going on in our lives to spend more than two hours in the church. Football games are more entertaining than worshipping the Almighty God who created the football players. Some men cannot sing, dance, or lift their hands to worship God, but they will jump, scream, and shout for a touchdown. Movies are more entertaining than fellowship with other brethren and receiving the supernatural power and peace of God.

We have sold our lives for big jobs and mortgages. Large homes and beautiful cars, though necessary, cannot comfort you or give you any peace when trouble arises. The message cannot last longer than noon, or the church will be empty. Do not be mistaken. You do not need to do exactly what they do in Africa, but humble yourself, and see the Lord is good. Try him with your time, attention, and possession, and see if he will not open your eyes to see his beauty and power, as there are no valid reasons not to.

"Better is one day in your court than a thousand elsewhere; I would rather be a doorkeeper in the house of my God than dwell in the tents of the wicked" (Ps. 84:10 NIV).

Rest for the Weary

"Come to me, all you who are weary and burdened, and I will give you rest. Take my yoke upon you and learn from me, for I am gentle and humble in heart, and you will find rest for your souls for my yoke is easy and my burden is light" (Matt. 11:28 NIV).

Cast all your fears upon Jesus Christ. God's power, wisdom, and peace are in store for you. This power does not come from running on a treadmill, lifting weights, eating salads, or watching Oprah and Dr. Phil. It comes from seeking the presence of God, obeying, and not grieving the Holy Spirit. Free yourself from the past, stay in your marriage, and listen to the Word of God. Love your wife and your children and fear God.

God told the children of Israel that he hates divorce. Rest in his presence. Let go of all your doubts, reasoning, and fears. Love and respect your spouse, and stop calling him or her names. What are you today that you did not receive from God? God sees that man as perfect and blameless. Begin to see and treat your spouse the way God sees him or her. Free yourself, give it all to him in his presence, and begin to listen and obey the Word.

Exchange your weakness for his strength, your sin for his righteousness, your anxiety for his peace, and your depression for his unspeakable joy. He has beauty for ashes and joy for mourning. As I complete the last chapters of this book, I cannot help but acknowledge how I have let God down at times in my life, how I have tried doing things my way to please others, and how I have solved problems how I've seen fit.

In the following days, the Holy Spirit spoke to me. "Therefore there is now no condemnation for those who are in Christ Jesus, because through Christ Jesus the law of the spirit who gives life has set you free from the law of sin and death" (Rom. 8:1–2 NIV).

Free yourself of all guilt and condemnation today, and receive life into your spirit, soul, and body through Jesus Christ, the soon coming king. Fight and drive the darkness out of your life, home, and neighborhood. Fight on your knees, find a Bible-believing church, study the Word of God, love others, and forgive people their offenses against you. God forgives you each day. Remember that you have done nothing to receive forgiveness and salvation from God. He has given it to you freely, so you need to forgive others unconditionally.

Finally, in the words of Paul the patriot,

> Therefore, I urge you, brothers, in view of God's mercy, to offer your bodies as living sacrifices, holy, and pleasing to God—this is your spiritual act of worship. Do not conform any longer to the pattern of this world, but be transformed by the renewing of your mind. Then you will be able to test and approve what God's will is—his good, pleasing and perfect will. (Rom. 12:1–2 NIV)

God loves you unconditionally. Celebrate the goodness and mercy of your God.

Chapter Seven

The Power of God

Uyo, Nigeria (1997)

It was around twelve thirty on a Friday afternoon. I was doing my tropical rotation (clinical rotation) in the department of obstetrics and gynecology at St. Luke's Hospital in Uyo. I had caught up with all my work, and I was not on call. I had been on call for five days since the previous Friday. The moment I said the word "TGIF," I had a message from a nurse in labor and delivery saying a lady was outside looking for me.

When I stepped outside, I met the receptionist of Faith Medical Center, a new privately owned nonprofit medical center owned by Church of God Mission International. She handed over a letter from Dr. Douglas, the physician who was the medical director. This medical center was less than six months old. I had been involved in setting it up from the first day. I had not been there for a week because of the workload at my tropical rotation. The letter read, "Treat as urgent. I need to see you immediately. Please do everything possible to see me within thirty minutes of getting this letter."

The receptionist refused to disclose what it was all about. When I got to the medical center, Dr. Douglas welcomed me as usual, offered me a glass of water, and asked me to sit down. I thought he was going to tell me not to stay away from the medical center as I had the past week, but he did not. He handed me a patient's medical record to review. In summary, it was about a forty-five-year-old man who had had an inguinal hernia repair at a local rural hospital in another town. His condition deteriorated three days after the first surgery, so he had a second operation.

When the surgeon went in the second time, he found a necrotic bowel, so he closed him back up and transferred him to a larger hospital in our city. He arrived at Faith Medical Center, five days after his first surgery. It was Friday afternoon. I needed some rest after being on call for five days out of seven, and I was supposed to be at my primary place of work. I had to go back to work as soon as possible, and I needed a good explanation for why I had been called to this medical center at this time.

"Why are you showing me this chart?"

"Listen first."

"Where is this patient?"

"Upstairs."

"I am an ob-gyn, so why are you calling me?"

"You need to calm down."

I was already on my feet, smiling and ready to go back to St. Luke's Hospital.

"Sit down and hear me out first."

"He was referred to a teaching hospital where they have several surgeons. What is he doing here?"

"I have asked the patient, Ubong, the same questions. He said Mr. Peter, a former patient of ours who was discharged from the medical center two months prior, brought him. Mr. Peter's aunt brought him here after his niece had been discharged from the hospital about four months prior to date."

The Miracle Medical Center

Mr. Ubong refused to go to the teaching hospital where he was referred to. He said he wanted to be treated in our hospital because he had heard it is a miracle medical center. His family was very dear to us, including Mr. Peter, his niece, and her parents, sister, and brothers. They all brought Mr. Ubong and did not want to hear about him going anywhere else.

I told Dr. Douglas, "Well, you have to find a surgeon to take care of him. This is way beyond my league." I made a second attempt to leave. I stood up from the chair and heard a loud snap.

"Dr. Otto, sit down! What is wrong with you?"

In the African culture, unfortunately there is sometimes no democracy in the practice of medicine or in the church. You have to be respectful and obedient to your elders, senior colleagues, and pastors. Dr. Douglas was also a deacon, teacher, and head of the Sunday schoolteachers' team in church. He was the pastor of our church when the leader was out of town. I had no choice but to obey the last command.

He said, "I want you to at least go and see him, hear his story, examine him, and come back so we can discuss what to do with him."

Reluctantly, I went to see Mr. Ubong. Mr. Peter, a cousin to Mr. Ubong, had been our patient in the past. He was brought to our hospital paralyzed from the waist down after he had fallen off the roof of a building. His coworkers, community, and another hospital had written him off as someone who would never walk again. After spending a month at our medical center, he began to regain function in his legs and practically walked out of the hospital with his legs. His niece was also cured of a deadly disease at our hospital.

When I walked into Mr. Ubong's room, I first introduced myself and asked what happened. After hearing his story, I told him that the best surgeon in town was at the teaching hospital that he was referred to. I also told him that there was no one to operate on him at our small medical center. I advised him to go to the teaching hospital for his surgery. He needed to be transported there to have surgery performed as soon as possible if there were any chance that he would survive.

Mr. Ubong said, "If I go to the teaching hospital, I am going to die. They require I pay a certain amount of money for the deposit. I will never have that kind of money. Besides, I have heard that God performs miracles here. My cousin would never have walked again if not for the power of God. I heard you guys are great surgeons. Your hospital is new, but in my hometown, they call it the miracle center. Sorry, Doctor. I am not going to any other hospital."

I left his room with one thought in my head. *May the God you are calling on stand by you.* I went over to Dr. Douglas and told him to find a surgeon to operate on his patient because he was not going anywhere.

Dr. Douglas said, "We were trained and certified as medical doctors and surgeons before you started specializing in obstetrics and gynecology. Have you done a bowel resection before?"

"Yes."

"Well, that man is not going anywhere. They have told him we have performed hundreds of surgeries with excellent results. We cannot let him die in our hospital. We have to operate on him."

Reluctantly, I went back to my primary place of work, took care of my patients, and handed over to the physician on call. I ate a late lunch and headed for our church missions hospital, nicknamed the "Miracle Center."

The Power of God

During the surgery, my medical staff and I were dazed. What we found was terrible and cannot be described in this book. We had to practically wash off the stool and debris. Over half of Mr. Ubong's intestines had sloughed off. Part of the small intestine ileum, all of the cecum, transverse colon, and proximal part of the descending colon had sloughed off. The remaining descending colon was buried in adhesions and inflammation and could not be mobilized for proper anastomosis. We consulted the best textbook of surgery available in our small medical library, completed bowel anastomosis on Mr. Ubong, and sent him to his room on IV fluids and antibiotics. If I were to describe in detail what was left in Mr. Ubong's abdomen for reconstruction, one would know that this man could only have survived by divine intervention.

On the third day after surgery, Mr. Ubong moved his bowels, and he was ready to eat. He was discharged from the hospital three weeks after my team and I performed surgery. He had no fistula (openings). He could tolerate all his meals, but he could not pay for half of the cost of his treatment, and this was a major worry for this man. 2 months after Mr. Ubong was discharged from the hospital, two dozen eggs were left in my house with a note to see Dr. Douglas for a message.

Sixty Dozen Eggs

The news was that Mr. Ubong had been to the hospital for his two-month checkup. He could not pay the hospital bill, but he brought us a gift. He brought sixty dozen eggs from his poultry farm. Dr. Douglas made sure that every family in church received at least an egg from Mr. Ubong. He shared the testimony of Mr. Ubong's faith and healing with members of the church to encourage them.

This is one miracle that God performed at Faith Medical Center. Dr. Douglas reminded me of some of the miracles God performed at this hospital when I visited with him in February 2012. He said, "If I never see another miracle in my life, I cannot forget the miracles God performed at Faith Medical Center."

He proceeded to discuss several patients who had been healed of many diseases. I was glad he did not remember how reluctant I was about performing surgery on Mr. Ubong. When I told him I was writing a book on the power of God, he reminded me of the man with insomnia and the devil's agent.

Insomnia

In his fifties, Mr. Thompson was a community leader, father, and successful businessman. I was seeing patients on a weekend at Faith Medical Center when I first met him. His medical problem seemed so easy to treat at first. His chief complaint was insomnia. He had not slept for two months. He had been to several doctors and pharmacists, but they could not find any medication to help put him to sleep. In my head, I said that this problem was easy to treat. When I asked him what medications had been prescribed to him in the past, he wrote down five different insomnia medications that he had been treated with, but he didn't have any good results.

He had not slept for over two months in spite of taking the medications separately and combining them against his doctors' recommendation. I decided to prescribe for him what I considered a stronger medication to help with his insomnia. He told me he had already tried it without any results. I mentioned the name of four other strong medications, and he knew them all. He said he had already seen a psychiatrist and been admitted to a psychiatric hospital for the treatment of insomnia without any improvement.

I did not know what else to do. I told him there was only one solution to his insomnia problem. He needed to go and see Reverend Eno of the Church of God Mission in Uyo for prayers. I had to tell him something to get him out of my office so I could see other patients.

Three weeks later, I saw Mr. Thompson in church on a Sunday morning. He told me that he became a member of Church of God Mission. His first day of sleep in over 2 months was in the church pews, the first day he visited the church. He started sleeping the day that Reverend Eno prayed for him. Is it not amazing what the power of God can do?

Chapter Eight

The Power of God

"And without faith it is impossible to please God, because anyone who comes to him must believe that he exists and that he rewards those who earnestly seek him" (Heb. 11:6 NIV).

Uyo, Nigeria (March 1997)

It was the end of a Sunday service. The assistant pastor stood at the podium to receive the third offering for the day. He said to the congregation, "Empty your wallets, give your best offering, challenge God, and see if he will not bless your finances."

People were going to the front of the church to give. Part of my mind believed God could do anything. The other part was very hesitant and thought this was a red flag, a pastor all out for money. What I had would not solve my problems anyway. I reluctantly removed the last money in my wallet, walked to the front of the church, and placed it in the offering box.

This was supposed to be money for a taxi to get back to my house. In addition, I had no food or groceries at home. There was no hope for lunch and supper that day or breakfast the following day. I could have probably bought some snacks for lunch, and that would have been all. Instead of keeping the money, I decided to give it in church in response to the pastor's message and call. In my head, all I could hear was, "You have been brainwashed, you are such a fool, and you came to the wrong church. This pastor is not right."

I shook off the thoughts and hung on to the man's words. Give the best you can, challenge God, and see if he will not reward you. After the benediction, I went downstairs along with other church members. In a split second, two different families offered me a ride home. I quickly accepted. On getting home, I drank some cold water from the refrigerator and went to my room to change up. I could not help but meditate on how good this God is and how he would fix my finances. I was doing my tropical rotation at St. Luke's Hospital at this time. I worked hard as a resident physician, saw several patients every day, and performed gynecological surgeries and at least twenty C-sections every month. My monthly stipend was less than a hundred dollars.

While in my bedroom changing into more comfortable clothes, I heard a knock on the door. The visitors were a family—a husband, wife, and two children. I had cared for the family during the pregnancy and delivery of both children. This time, both children were sick. It was a Sunday, and they did not want to wait for the pediatrician's office to open the following day. They also did not want to go wait in the emergency room for hours.

In Nigeria and other third-world countries, the doctors are trained and licensed to treat patients in at least five specialties: medicine, general surgery, obstetrics, gynecology, and pediatrics. They can specialize in any field if they choose to. They are also trained to refer to specialists if necessary. Sometimes, you could have one orthopedic surgeon for five million people. I quickly went inside my office and brought out my stethoscope and otoscope to examine both children.

The diagnosis was easy. I wrote prescriptions for both children. The couple was grateful. On the way out, he dipped his hands in his pocket and gave me a wad of cash. I was shocked and protested. He would not hear any of it. This was the beginning of something new.

How could one explain it? Up until this moment in my life, I knew how to give but not receive. In church, the pastor had preached that some of us give but do not know how to receive. He taught us that we should be humble enough to receive, or we will miss God's blessings. If we did not receive, we were robbing the giver of the opportunity to be blessed. Within sixty minutes of giving all my cash out in church, I had received fifteen times more than I started with that morning, sixty times more than what I gave at the last offering in the church. When the couple left, I sat on the couch mesmerized. Although I was a bachelor, I had other responsibilities. Other people depended on me for college tuition, rent, clothing, and food.

Before I could get up from the couch, the couple arrived again. They brought me enough groceries to last for three weeks. It was a miracle. I cooked a very delicious meal and invited my neighbors and colleagues to join me for dinner.

Before the Miracle

One week of fasting and prayer declared by the assistant pastor preceded the miracle above. His message prior to the week of fasting and prayer was, "If you need anything, write it down, read your Bible, fast and pray, and come to church daily at the close of work so we can pray together."

During the fast, his teaching was amazing. He taught us to trust God and his Word. We had to seek him with all our heart. "And without faith it is impossible to please God, because anyone who comes to him must believe that he exists and that he rewards those who earnestly seek him" (Heb. 11:6 NIV).

He taught us that God does not answer all prayers. He will answer prayers that are according to his will. "This is the confidence we have in approaching God: that if we ask anything according to his will, he hears us. And if we know that he hears us—whatever we ask—we know that we have what we asked of him" (1 John 5:14–15 NIV).

During the week, we were given chapters of the Bible to read, a few per day. Our faith gradually became strengthened, and some of us could receive answers to prayers. Giving has since become a part of my life. It does not have to be money. Sometimes, it is forgiving others, helping someone in need, and giving a small sacrifice and great reward. My finances were gradually transformed. A few weeks later, my monthly stipend was increased to five hundred dollars. To this date, the increase has not stopped because I have not stopped giving.

During my tropical rotation, I learned about service from the church. The training I received has been the foundation and underlying principle behind any business I venture into. I became one of the physicians or the one who was willing to treat the patients who had no money to pay for the hospital registration charge, physician fees, or medications. They could not pay me, but I can remember their gratitude and words: "God bless you."

The greatest prayer and reward that I received was from a group of people who kept reminding me that I was a bachelor. Their prayer was, "May God bless you with a good wife." It was not long before God answered that prayer. He sent me a beautiful and intelligent woman from South Dakota, and together, we have two amazing children.

Satan Is No Match for God
Uyo, Nigeria (1997)

There are thousands of books and stories all over the world on the power of the devil, vampires, voodoo, and witchcraft. Many of the stories are directed toward children and the youth. Not surprisingly, before a child reaches puberty, he or she is really brainwashed about the power of evil, monsters, ghosts, and witches. Many of these children have no knowledge of the power of God. During my childhood, I was told several stories about the devil and his agents. The argument is ongoing. Is God more powerful than the devil? I am a living witness of the manifestations of the power of God.

The Devil's Agent

This is one of the stories Dr. Douglas reminded me of when I visited him in February 2012. He was in the church when this incident happened in 1997, and he reminded me to include it in this book. I was in the church when the man who called himself the agent of the devil asked us to pray for him. It was the Sunday after a week of fasting and prayers. The pastor of our church stepped out to receive an offering from the church for a young man named Kofi who needed transportation money back to his home in northern Nigeria.

Kofi was about twenty-eight years old, and he told the story of his life to the whole church after we gave the offering for his transportation back home. He had suddenly appeared in the church in the middle of a service the previous evening. In his own words, he did not come in through the door or a window. He said he worked for Lucifer. Space, walls, or matter did not bind him and his fellow agents. His masters from another state sent him to suppress and quench the fire and power of God at our church.

He was sent there because there were too many activities going on in our church. The actions were disturbing their operation in the city of Uyo. Their masters were tired of the church blocking their operations through prayer and worship. He did not need to fly in an airplane or take a taxi to arrive at our church, so he did not come with money.

Our church was having twenty-one days of fasting, Bible teaching, and prayers. This man suddenly appeared in the church on day seven of the fasting and prayers. When he arrived in the church, the pastor was praying against the power of darkness. People were praying at the top of their voices with their eyes closed. They could not help but open their eyes when they heard noises and commotion in the church.

When they opened their eyes, they saw Kofi floating in the air and bouncing from wall to wall and from the ceiling to the floor without a trampoline or provocation. People were frightened and prayed more. The more they prayed, the more the man's speed and impact on the wall increased. This went on for more than an hour. Kofi was finally slammed on the floor from the ceiling. He said he was an agent from the kingdom of darkness. His mission was to come in and suppress the power of God without anyone in the church seeing him.

Unfortunately for him and fortunately for the church, he could not carry out his mission when he arrived. He lost his power and evil body that could walk through the wall. He became human, and the power of God slammed him from wall to wall. He said he had been working with his team for many years but had never experienced such failure. He could not get out of the church and go back to his master. The church members had stayed up all night praying and binding the works of darkness, and God answered their prayers. The church raised an offering to pay for his transportation back to his hometown in Kano, about five hundred miles from Uyo.

This incident strengthened our faith in God. In Exodus 7:10–12, God demonstrated his supremacy over the powers of darkness. God is faithful. He is our banner and victory. He fights all our battles, both seen and unseen. That is why Moses called him Jehovah Nissi, Lord our banner and victory. In Exodus 17:8–15, it reviews as follows.

> The Amalekites came and attacked the Israelites at Rephidim. Moses said to Joshua, "Choose some of our men and go out to fight the Amalekites. Tomorrow I will stand on top of the hill with the staff of God in my hands." So Joshua fought the Amalekites as Moses had ordered, and Moses, Aaron and Hur went to the top of the hill. As long as Moses held up his hands, the Israelites were winning, but whenever he lowered his hands, the Amalekites were winning. When Moses' hands grew tired, they took a stone and put it under him and he sat on it. Aaron and Hur held his hands up—one on one side, one on the other—so that his hands remained steady till sunset. So Joshua overcame the Amalekite army with the sword. Then the Lord said to Moses, "Write this on a scroll as something to be remembered and make sure that Joshua hears it, because I will completely blot out the name of Amalek from under heaven." Moses built an altar and called it The Lord is

my Banner. He said, "Because hands were lifted up against the throne of the Lord, the Lord will be at war against the Amalekites from generation to generation."

We have to remember that trusting God and obeying his commands brings great reward.

Raising the Dead

In the book of Matthew, a man approached Jesus to ask him to heal his son who was possessed by a demon. He was said to have seizures, the type that would cause him to fall into fires and water. His father brought him to Jesus's disciples, but they could not heal him. Jesus told his disciples that, if they have faith the size of a mustard seed, they would be able to perform great miracles and nothing would be impossible. He added, however, that this kind will only come out with prayer and fasting.

I once went to visit a friend whom I had met for the first time while I was a medical student. He had called me over the weekend needing help because he had eaten food with too much red pepper. He had developed diarrhea, but he described it as a fire coming out of his body. There was not much I could do for him except pray with him and joke about using ice to quench the fire. He was really miserable when I saw him. I was so busy at work that weekend that I did not give him much attention. During the week, I decided to visit him to make sure he was feeling better.

When I arrived at his home, I was told he had gone to church. I visited his church, and I was told that he had gone to raise the dead. I was shocked. John was a very funny guy. He was a Christian and writer for the town's local newspaper. His belief was so strong that, when he heard of the death of the mother of one member of his church, he forgot about his own illness. He rented a van, took with him some other church members, and traveled for twenty kilometers to raise the dead.

I could not help but go back the following weekend to look for my friend to hear his own version of raising the dead.

When I finally saw him, I first asked, "Did you raise the dead?"

"No, she did not make it."

John's courageous act has challenged my faith in many ways. At times, we meet people in hopeless situations. Instead of remembering that God said nothing shall be impossible if we asked, we tend to focus more on the problem. If John had the guts to go out to raise the dead, I have no excuse not to pray for my friends or individuals who abuse drugs and have other addictions. I am challenged not to give up on any situation.

This kind of faith comes by seeking God, studying his Word, and trusting him absolutely. God can use anybody. He can bring you from bankruptcy to financial stability. He will bless you with ideas that will help you to make wealth. He can heal you of any diseases. Remember that, without faith, it is impossible to please God. He rewards those who earnestly seek him. God loves you and me. He desires to have a relationship with us. He created us in his own image. Do not resist him today. Walking with God is not about a set of rules but a relationship. You have nothing to lose but rather too much to gain—peace, joy, strength, wisdom, and security in this world and eternal life. Do not walk alone. Taste and see that the Lord is good.

Chapter Nine

I Am Omnipowerful

If you are blessed to experience for one minute the true presence, love, and power of God, you will be changed forever. You will be in awe of who he is and will hunger to be left in his presence for the rest of your life. I once had a conversation with a medical student at a teaching hospital in North Carolina. I asked this student what she did in her spare time to cope with stress. She said she played music, jogged, exercised, ate food, and went to the synagogue. When I asked her which of the activities was most beneficial in reducing stress, she said it was going to the synagogue.

I became very curious to know what she did in the synagogue to reduce stress. She told me that they did not sing songs like I did in my contemporary Christian church. She said they read and meditated on the Word of God all the time.

The most interesting part of the conversation came when I asked her a particular question. "What is God's real name? I have heard so many versions. Is it Jehovah, Yaweh, Jehovah Rapha, or El-Shaddai? Is it Jehovah Nissi, Jehovah Tsikenu, Elohim, El Olam, or Adonai?"

She closed her eyes in thought. When she opened her eyes, she gave me the most confusing answer. "We do not know his name."

"What?"

In my own ignorance, I thought, *Wow. She is probably lying to me about the synagogue.*

I have read many versions of the Bible five times over, most of the time with concordance. To be sure I was not being lied to, I felt it was necessary to test the young woman's knowledge of the Bible, which was uncontestable. After answering all of the questions, she knew then that I was ready for the right answer, so she went back to the original question.

"What is God's real name?"

"God is so limitless, infinite, loving, powerful, unique, and diverse such that nobody is able to describe him or give him a name."

"How about Yaweh and Jehovah, Lord, God, and all the other names that I know in Hebrew and Greek?"

"Men have tried to describe him throughout the ages based on a glimpse or speck of the experience or revelation they received from God at different times. The men who have had a glimpse of his love, ability, and power have been so mesmerized that they came up with different descriptions of him. That is why we have so many names for Jehovah God. The Holy Spirit who revealed God to men and women over the ages helped them to give near descriptions of how they experienced God."

Her next answer was shocking but true.

"God, when Moses asked what his name was, came up with a near-perfect description of him. The best words he could say to make some meaning to Moses was, 'I am who I am.' God said, 'I am the same yesterday, today, and forever. I am your peace, your father, your provider, your shepherd, your future, your tomorrow, your anchor, your shield, your healer, your justifier, your righteousness, and your comforter, light, and salvation.' Relax in his arms, and trust in the great I am."

Shalom.

About the Author

Dr. Otto Umana, a native of Nigeria, immigrated to the United States in 1999 to complete his medical education. He is a member of Solid Rock Assembly of God in Columbus, Georgia, and is a physician. Dr. Umana and his wife, Kari, are independent medical missionaries who are passionate about helping the poor; Dr. Umana has helped establish two missionary hospitals in Nigeria.